Afternoon tea

PARTY

High tea delights with sugar and spice

THE AUSTRALIAN
Women's Weekly

contents

Slow down and savour the finer things in life with good friends and a pot of your favourite tea. Here's your chance to spoil yourself with cucumber sandwiches, smoked salmon, scones, lamingtons, melting moments and chocolate slice. Teatime will be your favourite time.

Editorial & Food Director

Pamela Clark

Australian cup and spoon measurements are metric. A conversion chart appears on page 77.

Chai

Types of tea

Earl Grey

All about tea

Tea has a rich and diverse history that dates back hundreds of years and spans countries all over the world. The traditions and ceremonies that have developed around the drinking of tea are fascinating and varied, often reflecting the culture of their origin. But regardless of its history, where it is enjoyed, whether it is green, black, medicinal, a blend or a herbal infusion, tea brings us together, revitalises and warms us.

In London, as early as the 1700s, it became popular to serve tea and entertain guests in one's home. With tea drinking embraced as a social activity, it didn't take long for the art of afternoon tea to be perfected. Scones, pastries, sandwiches and cakes accompanied black tea with milk, carefully brewed to create the finest possible cup.

Loose-leaf teas

Today, we embrace many kinds of tea. Although tea bags are still the most commonly bought, loose-leaf teas are making a comeback. The true flavour of a tea can really be tasted when you brew with loose leaves.

How to brew
THE PERFECT CUP

- Use loose leaves. They're almost always better quality.

- Fill the kettle with fresh, cold water and bring it to the boil (once only, to maintain the water's oxygen).

- Preheat the teapot by swilling hot water around in it. Pour it out, and then replace the lid.

- Know how many cups the teapot holds so you can get the ratio of water to tea right. Add one teaspoon of tea per person and one for the teapot. As a guide, it's usually best to fill the teapot to near the base of the spout.

- If making black or herbal tea, carry the teapot to the just-boiled kettle, and pour the water in immediately. Replace the lid straight away to retain the heat. Green tea is better brewed with water that is just off the boil, to avoid bitterness.

- Depending on the variety of tea, and whether the leaves are broken or whole, black tea is best brewed for 3 to 5 minutes; green and herbal teas are best brewed for 2 to 4 minutes.

- Milk or lemon can be added to black tea, along with sugar, if desired. Honey or mint are often added to green and herbal tea varieties.

- Milk first? Or tea first? Neither is incorrect, however the taste of the tea will differ. The fats in milk won't overheat if you slowly pour hot tea onto cold milk. However, some say that pouring a small amount of cold milk into a large cup of hot tea imparts a stale taste. But others prefer adding milk afterwards, because it's easier to gauge the desired amount. So, milk first or last? It's really up to you.

savoury

There's no better place to start your tea party than with a lavish selection of sandwiches and moreish finger food.

Tip Swap smoked salmon for smoked trout or try hot smoked salmon or trout

salmon & herb cream cheese sandwiches

- 330g (2 ounces) cream cheese, softened
- 1 teaspoon each finely chopped fresh dill and fresh chives
- 1 teaspoon lemon juice
- 1 teaspoon rinsed, drained baby capers, chopped finely
- 4 slices white bread (180g), crusts removed
- 125g (4 ounces) smoked salmon
- 4 large rocket leaves (arugula), trimmed

1 Combine cream cheese, dill, chives, juice and capers in a small bowl. Season to taste.

2 Using a rolling pin, roll over one slice of bread to flatten slightly. Spread with a quarter of the cream cheese mixture; top with a quarter of the smoked salmon and one rocket leaf, roll tightly to enclose filling.

3 Repeat with remaining bread, cream cheese mixture, smoked salmon and rocket. Trim ends then slice each roll into four circles.

makes 16
prep time 20 minutes

trout & asparagus frittata with rocket pesto

- 18 asparagus spears (340g), trimmed
- 150g (4½ ounces) sliced smoked ocean trout, chopped coarsely
- ¼ cup (20g) finely grated parmesan
- 6 eggs
- ⅔ cup (160ml) pouring cream

rocket pesto
- 45g (1½ ounces) baby rocket (arugula) leaves
- 2 tablespoons roasted pine nuts
- 1 clove garlic, chopped coarsely
- 2 tablespoons finely grated parmesan
- ¼ cup (60ml) olive oil
- 1 tablespoon lemon juice

1 Preheat oven to 180°C/360°F. Oil a six-hole (¾-cup/180ml) texas muffin pan; line bases with baking paper.
2 Cut asparagus into 4cm (1½-inch) lengths; reserve asparagus tips. Layer remaining asparagus, trout and parmesan in pan holes. Whisk eggs and cream in a medium bowl; pour into pan holes. Top each frittata with three asparagus tips.
3 Bake frittatas about 25 minutes. Stand in pan 5 minutes; using a palette knife, loosen frittatas from edge of pan before turning out, top-side up.

4 Meanwhile, make rocket pesto.
5 Serve frittatas with rocket pesto.

rocket pesto Blend or process rocket, nuts, garlic and parmesan until finely chopped. With motor operating, gradually add combined oil and juice in a thin, steady stream; process until pesto is smooth.

makes 6
prep + cook time
40 minutes

Tip Pesto can be made a day ahead,
place plastic wrap on surface to stop
air from discolouring the pesto. Cover
tightly and refrigerate until required.

tip Chicken mixture can be prepared a day ahead; store, covered, in the fridge. Freeze unbaked pies in the patty pans. To cook from frozen, add 10-15 minutes to the cooking time.

mini chicken & leek pies

- 1 cup (250ml) chicken stock
- 170g (5½ ounces) chicken breast fillet
- 1 tablespoon olive oil
- 1 small leek (200g), sliced thinly
- ½ stalk celery (75g), trimmed, chopped finely
- 2 teaspoons plain (all-purpose) flour
- 2 teaspoons fresh thyme leaves
- ¼ cup (60ml) pouring cream
- 1 teaspoon wholegrain mustard
- 2 sheets shortcrust pastry
- 1 sheet puff pastry
- 1 egg yolk
- 2 teaspoons sesame seeds

makes 16
prep + cook time
1 hour 20 minutes

1 Bring stock to the boil in a small saucepan over high heat. Add chicken; return to the boil. Reduce heat to low; simmer, covered, for 10 minutes or until chicken is cooked through. Remove from heat; stand chicken in poaching liquid 10 minutes. Remove chicken; chop finely. Reserve ¼ cup of the poaching liquid; discard remainder.

2 Heat oil in a medium saucepan over medium heat; cook leek and celery, stirring, for 5 minutes or until leek softens. Add flour and half the thyme; cook, stirring, 1 minute. Gradually stir in reserved liquid and cream; cook, stirring, until mixture boils and thickens. Stir in chicken and mustard; season to taste. Cool 10 minutes.

3 Preheat oven to 220°C/425°F. Oil 16 holes of two 12-hole (2-tablespoon/40ml) flat-based patty pans.

4 Cut 16 x 7cm (2¾-inch) rounds from shortcrust pastry; press one round into each of the prepared holes. Spoon 1 tablespoon chicken mixture into each pastry case. Cut 16 x 6cm (2½-inch) rounds from puff pastry; top chicken pies with puff pastry lids. Brush lids with yolk; sprinkle with remaining thyme and sesame seeds. Using a sharp knife, make two small slits in each lid. Bake, uncovered, for 20 minutes or until browned lightly.

creamy egg & watercress sandwiches

- 3 eggs
- ¼ cup (75g) mayonnaise
- 1 teaspoon dijon mustard
- 1 tablespoon each finely chopped fresh chives and fresh flat-leaf parsley
- 30g (1 ounce) butter, softened
- 8 slices white bread (360g)
- 1 cup (20g) loosely packed watercress sprigs

1 Boil eggs in a medium saucepan of water for 6 minutes or until hard. Cool, then peel and coarsely mash eggs with a fork.

2 Combine egg, mayonnaise, mustard and herbs in a medium bowl. Season to taste.

3 Butter bread slices; sandwich egg mixture and watercress between bread slices. Discard crusts; cut each sandwich into four fingers.

tips Use a whole-egg mayonnaise as it has a creamy texture. Swap watercress for your favourite leafy green; rocket (arugula) or endive would both work well as they have a slightly bitter taste.

tip If you don't have enough oven trays to bake the pizzas, roll out the dough on sheets of baking paper and carefully transfer the paper with the pizzas to hot trays (from the previous batch). You may need to reduce the cooking time by a few minutes.

tomato, pancetta & buffalo mozzarella pizza

- 1 cup (250ml) barbecue sauce
- 250g (8 ounces) mixed baby heirloom tomatoes, halved
- 10 slices pancetta (150g), torn roughly
- 3 balls buffalo mozzarella (420g), drained, torn
- 1 cup loosely packed small fresh basil leaves

pizza dough
- 1½ cups (375ml) warm milk
- 2 teaspoons (7g) dried yeast
- 1 tablespoon honey
- 4 cups (600g) plain (all-purpose) flour
- 1 teaspoon salt
- ¼ cup (60ml) extra virgin olive oil

1 Make pizza dough.
2 Preheat oven to 220°C/425°F. Line oven trays with baking paper.
3 Divide pizza dough into 40 balls. Roll each ball on a lightly floured surface into 6cm (2½-inch) rounds. Place pizza bases on oven trays (see tip).
4 Spread 1 teaspoon sauce over each pizza base. Divide tomatoes, pancetta and mozzarella between bases. Bake pizzas, in batches, for 15 minutes or until bases are crisp and mozzarella is melted.
5 Sprinkle pizzas with basil. Serve immediately.

pizza dough Combine milk, yeast and honey in a small bowl. Stand for 5 minutes or until foamy. Combine flour and salt in a large bowl; make a well in the centre, add yeast mixture and oil. Using your hands, mix until combined. Turn dough onto a lightly floured surface; knead for 10 minutes or until dough is smooth and elastic. Place in an oiled bowl, turn to coat in oil. Cover with plastic wrap; stand in a warm, draught-free place for 1 hour or until dough has doubled in size.

makes 40
prep + cook time
45 minutes (+ standing)

chicken & almond sandwiches

- 1 cup (250ml) chicken stock
- 1 cup (250ml) water
- 6 whole black peppercorns
- 1 bay leaf
- 250g (8 ounces) chicken breast fillet
- 1 stalk celery (150g), trimmed, chopped finely
- 2 tablespoons flaked almonds, roasted
- ¼ cup (60g) crème fraîche
- 2 tablespoons mayonnaise
- 1 teaspoon lemon juice
- 2 teaspoons finely chopped fresh tarragon
- 30g (1 ounce) butter, softened
- 8 slices light rye bread (360g)

1 Combine stock, the water, peppercorns, bay leaf and chicken in a small saucepan; bring to the boil over medium heat. Reduce heat to low; simmer, uncovered, for 15 minutes or until chicken is cooked through, turning chicken halfway through cooking time. Remove chicken from poaching liquid. When cool enough to handle, chop chicken finely.
2 Combine chicken in a medium bowl with celery, nuts, crème fraîche, mayonnaise, juice and tarragon. Season to taste.
3 Butter bread slices; sandwich chicken mixture between bread slices. Discard crusts; cut each sandwich into three fingers, then cut each in half crossways.

tips To save time, use leftover chicken or bought barbecue chicken; remove all skin and bones before using. Tarragon is the essential flavouring for many classic French sauces and dishes. It is also blended with parsley, chives and chervil to make *fines herbes*.

makes 24
prep + cook time
35 minutes (+ cooling)

smoked salmon & cream cheese stacks

- **250g (8 ounces) cream cheese, softened**
- **½ cup (120g) sour cream**
- **2 tablespoons lemon juice**
- **2 tablespoons finely chopped fresh dill**
- **2 teaspoons coarsely chopped baby capers**
- **1 teaspoon finely grated lemon rind**
- **300g (9½ ounces) sliced smoked salmon**

1 Oil six holes of a 12-hole (⅓-cup/80ml) muffin pan; line with plastic wrap.

2 Beat cheese, sour cream and juice in a small bowl with an electric mixer until smooth. Stir in dill, capers and rind.

3 Cut 12 x 6cm (2½-inch) rounds and 12 x 7cm (2¾-inch) rounds from salmon slices. Place one small salmon round in base of each pan hole; top with 1 tablespoon of cream cheese mixture. Layer with remaining small salmon rounds and another 1 tablespoon of cream cheese mixture. Repeat with larger rounds and remaining cream cheese mixture, finishing with salmon.

4 Cover pan with plastic wrap; refrigerate 1 hour. Remove stacks from pan; carefully remove plastic wrap. Serve salmon stacks, top-side down.

tip If salmon slices are less than 6cm wide, you can use two pieces side by side. Overlap edges of salmon then press them together gently before cutting out rounds.

serving suggestion Serve with rocket salad and lime wedges.

Tip For even, thin slices, use a vegetable peeler to slice the cucumber.

marinated cucumber sandwiches

- 2 lebanese cucumbers (260g), peeled, sliced thinly lengthways
- 1 tablespoon white wine vinegar
- 1 tablespoon finely chopped fresh dill
- ½ teaspoon sea salt flakes
- ½ teaspoon caster (superfine) sugar
- ¼ teaspoon cracked black pepper
- 30g (1 ounce) butter, softened
- 8 slices wholemeal bread (360g)
- ½ cup (120g) crème fraîche

1 Combine cucumber, vinegar, dill, salt, sugar and pepper in a medium bowl. Cover; refrigerate 2 hours, then drain cucumber. Discard excess liquid.

2 Butter bread slices. Spread crème fraîche over half the bread slices, then top with cucumber and remaining bread. Discard crusts; cut each sandwich into four fingers.

makes 16
prep time 20 minutes (+ refrigeration)

za'atar pizza

- 430g (14-ounce) loaf turkish bread
- 2 tablespoons extra virgin olive oil
- 2 tablespoons fresh flat-leaf parsley leaves
- 1½ cups (420g) Greek-style yoghurt

za'atar mixture

- ½ teaspoon sumac
- ¼ teaspoon salt
- 2 tablespoons za'atar
- ¼ cup olive oil

1 Preheat oven to 240°C/475°F.

2 Combine ingredients for za'atar mixture in a small bowl.

3 Cut bread in half horizontally. Spread za'atar mixture over cut halves. Place bread on an oven tray; bake for 7 minutes.

4 Drizzle pizza with oil; cut into 12 triangles. Sprinkle with parsley; serve with yoghurt.

tips Za'atar is a mix of sumac, sesame seeds, salt and thyme. It is available from Middle-Eastern delis and major supermarkets. Make pizza up to 4 hours ahead; reheat in a slow (150°C/300°F) oven.

makes 24
prep + cook time
15 minutes

roasted beetroot & red onion dip

- 5 medium beetroot (800g), trimmed
- 1 medium bulb garlic (70g)
- 2 medium red onions (340g), quartered
- 1 tablespoon fresh thyme leaves
- cooking-oil spray
- 1½ cups (360g) sour cream
- 1 cup (100g) walnuts, toasted
- 1 tablespoon red wine vinegar

1 Preheat oven to 180°C/350°F. Line an oven tray with baking paper.

2 Place beetroot, garlic, onion and thyme on oven tray. Spray with cooking oil; season. Bake for 1 hour. Remove garlic, onion and thyme from tray. Cover beetroot with foil; bake for a further 45 minutes or until tender. When cool enough to handle, remove and discard skins. Chop beetroot coarsely.

3 Squeeze garlic cloves from bulb. Blend or process beetroot with garlic, onion, thyme, sour cream, nuts and vinegar until smooth. Season to taste.

serving suggestion
Serve with pan-fried pitta, turkish bread fingers, crackers or crudités.

Tip Swap multigrain for your preferred bread.

smoked trout ribbon sandwiches

- **⅓ cup (100g) mayonnaise**
- **1 teaspoon finely grated lemon rind**
- **2 teaspoons lemon juice**
- **1 tablespoon finely chopped fresh chives**
- **8 slices multigrain bread (360g)**
- **140g (5 ounces) skinless smoked trout, flaked finely**

1 Combine mayonnaise, rind, juice and chives in a small bowl.

2 Spread bread with mayonnaise mixture. Sandwich trout between bread slices. Discard crusts; cut each sandwich into three fingers.

makes 12
prep time 10 minutes

prosciutto & roasted capsicum quiche

- 6 slices prosciutto (90g)
- 3 sheets ready-rolled shortcrust pastry
- 4 slices (170g) bottled roasted red capsicum, chopped coarsely
- ⅓ cup coarsely chopped fresh basil
- ¾ cup (75g) pizza cheese

quiche filling
- 300ml pouring cream
- ¼ cup (60ml) milk
- 3 eggs

1 Preheat oven to 200°C/400°F. Oil a 12-hole (⅓-cup/80ml) muffin pan.
2 Cook prosciutto in a heated oiled large frying pan over medium heat for 1 minute each side or until crisp. Cool; chop coarsely.
3 Cut 12 x 9cm (3¾-inch) rounds from pastry; press into pan holes. Divide combined prosciutto, capsicum, basil and cheese among pastry cases.
4 Make quiche filling.
5 Pour quiche filling into pastry cases. Bake quiches about 25 minutes. Stand in pan 5 minutes before serving.

quiche filling Whisk ingredients in a large jug.

tips Quiches can be frozen for up to 2 months. Thaw in fridge overnight; reheat in oven until heated through. Prosciutto is a dry-cured ham that is usually sold in thin slices.

makes 16
prep time 25 minutes

Tip Limes can be expensive when they aren't in season so make the aïoli with lemons instead.

prawn sandwiches with lime & pepper aïoli

- 16 medium cooked king prawns (shrimp) (720g)
- 30g (1 ounce) butter, softened
- 8 slices white bread (360g)
- 1 cup (60g) shredded baby cos (romaine) lettuce

lime & pepper aïoli

- ½ cup (150g) mayonnaise
- 1 small clove garlic, crushed
- ½ teaspoon finely grated lime rind
- 2 teaspoons lime juice
- ¼ teaspoon cracked black pepper

1 Make aïoli.
2 Shell and devein prawns; halve lengthways. Stir prawns into aïoli. Season to taste.
3 Butter bread slices; sandwich prawn mixture and lettuce between bread slices. Discard crusts; cut each sandwich into four triangles.

lime & pepper aïoli
Combine ingredients in a medium bowl.

Tip Mustard dogs can be assembled a day ahead; store, covered, in the fridge. Alternatively, freeze for up to 2 weeks. To cook from frozen, bake for 25 minutes.

mustard dogs in pastry

- 2 sheets puff pastry
- ½ cup (140g) wholegrain mustard
- 1 cup (120g) finely grated cheddar
- 6 American-style hot dogs (390g), halved crossways
- 1 egg, beaten lightly
- 2 tablespoons poppy seeds

1 Preheat oven to 220°C/425°F. Line a large oven tray with baking paper.
2 Cut each pastry sheet into 3 x 8cm (3¼-inch) lengths; halve each length crossways into rectangles.
3 Spread 2 teaspoons mustard over each rectangle, sprinkle with 1 tablespoon cheddar; leave a 1cm (½-inch) border down one short side. Place one hot dog half over mustard and cheddar; roll up tightly.

4 Place mustard dogs, seam-side down, on oven tray, brush with egg; sprinkle with poppy seeds.
5 Bake for 15 minutes or until pastry is puffed and golden. Serve immediately.

makes 12
prep + cook time
35 minutes

sweet

You can never be too generous when it comes to sweet treats. Pick and choose a variety that take your fancy.

Tip You can use just one type of jam for this recipe, but we like the variety of flavours using different jams.

jam tarts

- 2 cups (300g) plain (all-purpose) flour
- ¼ cup (40g) icing (confectioners') sugar
- 185g (6 ounces) cold unsalted butter, chopped coarsely
- 1 egg yolk
- 1 tablespoon iced water, approximately
- ⅓ cup (110g) each strawberry, black cherry, apricot and raspberry jam
- 1 tablespoon icing (confectioners') sugar, extra

1 Process flour, icing sugar and butter until crumbly. With motor operating, add egg yolk and enough of the water to make ingredients come together. Turn dough onto a floured surface; knead gently until smooth. Roll half the pastry between sheets of baking paper until 3mm (⅛-inch) thick. Repeat with remaining pastry. Place on trays; refrigerate 30 minutes.

2 Grease three 12-hole (1-tablespoon/20ml) shallow round-based patty pans.

3 Using a 6cm (2½-inch) round cutter, cut 18 rounds from each piece of pastry; re-roll pastry scraps as necessary. Press pastry rounds into pan holes. Prick pastry cases well with a fork. Refrigerate 30 minutes.

4 Preheat oven to 220°C/425°F.

5 Bake pastry cases about 5 minutes. Drop slightly rounded teaspoons of jam into pastry cases.

6 Bake tarts about 10 minutes; cool. Dust with extra sifted icing sugar before serving.

raspberry & white chocolate friands

- 6 egg whites
- 185g (6 ounces) butter, melted
- 1 cup (120g) ground almonds
- 1½ cups (240g) icing (confectioners') sugar
- ½ cup (75g) plain (all-purpose) flour
- 100g (3 ounces) white chocolate, chopped coarsely
- 100g (3 ounces) fresh or frozen raspberries
- 1 teaspoon icing (confectioners') sugar, extra

1 Preheat oven to 180°C/350°F. Grease eight ½-cup (125ml) rectangular friand pans; stand on an oven tray.
2 Place egg whites in a medium bowl; whisk lightly with a fork until combined. Add butter, ground almonds, sifted icing sugar and flour, and chocolate. Using a wooden spoon, stir until just combined. Divide mixture between pans.
3 Bake friands 10 minutes; top with raspberries. Bake a further 15 minutes. Turn, top-side up, onto a wire rack to cool.
4 Serve friands warm, or at room temperature, dusted with extra sifted icing sugar.

tips Use frozen berries unthawed to minimise their colour bleeding into the mixture. Friands are at their best served on the day of baking, but they can be stored in an airtight container for 2 days, or frozen for up to 3 months.

makes 8
prep + cook time
45 minutes

makes 22
prep + cook time
30 minutes

lemon madeleines

- 2 eggs
- 2 tablespoons caster (superfine) sugar
- 2 tablespoons icing (confectioners') sugar
- 2 teaspoons finely grated lemon rind
- ¼ cup (35g) plain (all-purpose) flour
- ¼ cup (35g) self-raising flour
- 75g (2½ ounces) unsalted butter, melted
- 1 tablespoon lemon juice
- 2 tablespoons icing (confectioners') sugar, extra

1 Preheat oven to 200°C/400°F. Grease 22 holes of two 12-hole (1½-tablespoon/30ml) madeleine trays.
2 Beat eggs, caster sugar, icing sugar and rind in a small bowl with an electric mixer for 8 minutes or until pale and thick.
3 Meanwhile, triple-sift flours; sift flour over egg mixture. Pour butter and juice down the side of the bowl then fold ingredients together.
4 Drop rounded tablespoons of mixture into pan holes.

5 Bake madeleines about 10 minutes. Tap hot pan firmly on bench to release madeleines; turn immediately onto baking-paper-covered wire racks to cool.
6 Serve dusted with extra sifted icing sugar.

tips Madeleines are best served on the day of baking. Cover and store in an airtight container for 1 day or freeze for up to 1 month. Swap lemon for orange or lime for a citrus twist.

ring of roses cupcakes

- 90g (3 ounces) butter, softened
- 1 teaspoon vanilla extract
- ½ cup (110g) caster (superfine) sugar
- 2 eggs
- 1 cup (150g) self-raising flour
- 2 tablespoons milk
- yellow, white and pink edible sugar roses

butter cream

- 90g (3 ounces) butter, softened
- 1 cup (240g) icing (confectioners') sugar
- 1 tablespoon milk

1 Preheat oven to 180°C/350°F. Line eight holes of a 12-hole (⅓-cup/80ml) muffin pan with paper cases.

2 Beat butter, extract, sugar, eggs, sifted flour and milk in a small bowl with an electric mixer on low speed until ingredients are combined. Increase speed to medium; beat until mixture has changed to a paler colour. Drop ¼-cups of mixture into paper cases.

3 Bake cupcakes about 20 minutes. Stand cakes in pan 5 minutes before turning, top-side up, onto a wire rack to cool.

4 Make butter cream.

5 Spread cold cakes with butter cream. Position a circle of yellow, white or pink sugar roses in centre of each cake.

butter cream Beat butter in a small bowl with an electric mixer until as white as possible; beat in sifted icing sugar and milk, in two batches.

makes 8
prep + cook time
40 minutes

makes 12
prep + cook time
1 hour (+ cooling)

Yummy!

Tips Use any fresh berries you like. If you only have one patty pan, bake the first batch, then wash, grease and flour the pan again before baking the next batch.

mulberry powder puffs

- **2 eggs**
- **⅓ cup (75g) caster (superfine) sugar**
- **2 tablespoons cornflour (cornstarch)**
- **2 tablespoons plain (all-purpose) flour**
- **2 tablespoons self-raising flour**
- **½ cup (125ml) thickened (heavy) cream**
- **2 tablespoons icing (confectioners') sugar**
- **½ cup (70g) finely chopped fresh mulberries**

1 Preheat oven to 180°C/350°F. Grease and flour two 12-hole (1-tablespoons/20ml) shallow round-based patty pans.

2 Beat eggs and caster sugar in a small bowl with an electric mixer for 5 minutes or until thick and creamy. Sift flours twice onto baking paper, then sift over egg mixture; fold flour into egg mixture.

3 Drop level tablespoons of mixture into pan holes. Bake puffs about 12 minutes; turn immediately onto wire racks to cool.

4 To make mulberry cream, beat cream and half the sifted icing sugar in a small bowl with an electric mixer until soft peaks form; fold in berries.

5 Sandwich puffs with mulberry cream just before serving. Dust with sifted remaining icing sugar.

rosewater meringue kisses

- 2 egg whites
- ½ cup (110g) caster (superfine) sugar
- 1 teaspoon rosewater
- pink food colouring
- 2 tablespoons pouring cream
- 90g (3 ounces) white chocolate, chopped finely
- 4 fresh or thawed frozen raspberries

1 Preheat oven to 120°C/250°F. Grease oven trays; line with baking paper.

2 Beat egg whites, sugar, rosewater and a few drops of pink colouring in a small bowl with an electric mixer for 10 minutes or until sugar is dissolved.

3 Spoon mixture into a piping bag fitted with a 2cm (¾-inch) fluted tube; pipe 4cm (1½-inch) stars, about 2cm (¾-inch) apart, onto oven trays. Bake meringues for 50 minutes or until dry to touch. Cool on trays.

4 Meanwhile, bring cream to the boil in a small saucepan. Remove from heat; add chocolate, stir until smooth. Push raspberries through a fine sieve over a bowl to make raspberry purée. Stir raspberry purée into chocolate with a few drops of pink food colouring. Refrigerate for 20 minutes or until filling is spreadable.

5 Sandwich meringues with filling.

Tips The cake is easier to handle if it's a day old. Sponge or butter cake can be used. Fill the lamingtons with jam and cream, if desired.

lamingtons

- 6 eggs
- ⅔ cup (150g) caster (superfine) sugar
- ⅓ cup (50g) cornflour (cornstarch)
- ½ cup (75g) plain (all-purpose) flour
- ⅓ cup (50g) self-raising flour
- 2 cups (160g) desiccated coconut, approximately

chocolate icing
- 3 cups (500g) icing (confectioners') sugar
- ½ cup (50g) cocoa powder
- 15g (½ ounce) butter, melted
- ⅔ cup (160ml) milk

1 Preheat oven to 180°C/350°F. Grease a deep 23cm (9-inch) square cake pan.
2 Beat eggs in a medium bowl with an electric mixer for 10 minutes or until thick and creamy. Gradually beat in sugar, beat until sugar dissolves after each addition. Fold in triple-sifted flours. Spread mixture into pan.
3 Bake cake about 30 minutes. Turn cake, top-side up, onto a wire rack to cool.

4 Make chocolate icing.
5 Cut cake into squares. Dip squares in icing, drain off excess; toss squares in coconut. Place lamingtons on a wire rack to set.

chocolate icing Sift icing sugar and cocoa into a large heatproof bowl; stir in butter and milk. Stir icing over a large saucepan of simmering water until of a coating consistency.

chocolate hazelnut cupcakes

- ¼ cup (25g) cocoa powder
- ¼ cup (60ml) hot water
- 100g (3½ ounces) dark (semi-sweet) chocolate, melted
- 100g (3½ ounces) butter, melted
- 1 cup (220g) firmly packed brown sugar
- ¾ cup (75g) ground hazelnuts
- 3 eggs, separated
- 2 tablespoons colourful sprinkles

white chocolate ganache

- ¾ cup (180ml) pouring cream
- 540g (1 pound) white chocolate, chopped coarsely

1 Preheat oven to 180°C/350°F. Line a 12-hole (⅓-cup/80ml) muffin pan with paper cases.

2 Blend cocoa with the water in a medium bowl until smooth. Stir in chocolate, butter, sugar, nuts and egg yolks.

3 Beat egg whites in a small bowl with an electric mixer until soft peaks form; fold into chocolate mixture in two batches. Fill paper cases three-quarters full.

4 Bake cakes 25 minutes. Stand cakes in pan 5 minutes before turning, top-side up, onto a wire rack to cool.

5 Make white chocolate ganache.

6 Spoon ganache into a large piping bag fitted with a large plain tube. Pipe large swirls of ganache onto cooled cakes. Sprinkle with sprinkles.

white chocolate ganache

Bring cream to the boil in small saucepan; remove from heat. When bubbles subside, add chocolate; stir until smooth. Transfer mixture to small bowl. Cover; refrigerate 30 minutes. Beat with an electric mixer until light and fluffy.

makes 12
prep + cook time 50 minutes
(+ refrigeration)

Tip You can use hundreds and thousands or confetti sprinkles to decorate the cakes.

buttermilk scones

- 2½ cups (375g) self-raising flour
- 1 tablespoon caster (superfine) sugar
- ¼ teaspoon salt
- 30g (1 ounce) butter, chopped
- 1¼ cups (310ml) buttermilk, approximately

makes 25
prep + cook time 35 minutes

1 Preheat oven to 240°C/475°F. Grease a deep 19cm (8-inch) square cake pan.
2 Place flour, sugar and salt in a large bowl; rub in butter with fingertips. Make a well in centre of flour mixture; add buttermilk. Using a knife, cut buttermilk through flour mixture to mix to a soft, sticky dough.
3 Knead dough quickly and lightly on a floured surface until smooth. Press dough out evenly to 2cm (¾-inch) thickness. Dip a 4.5cm (1¾-inch) round cutter into flour; cut as many rounds as you can from dough.

4 Place scones side by side, just touching, in pan. Gently knead scraps of dough together; repeat pressing and cutting out of dough. Place rounds in pan; brush tops with a little milk.
5 Bake scones about 15 minutes.

serving suggestion
Serve with jam and cream.

caramel choc-chip mud cakes

- 90g (3 ounces) white chocolate, chopped coarsely
- 90g (3 ounces) unsalted butter, chopped coarsely
- ½ cup (110g) firmly packed brown sugar
- 2 tablespoons golden syrup or treacle
- ½ cup (125ml) milk
- ¾ cup (110g) plain (all-purpose) flour
- ¼ cup (35g) self-raising flour
- 1 egg
- 2 tablespoons milk Choc Bits
- 2 teaspoons icing (confectioners') sugar

1 Preheat oven to 160°C/325°F. Grease eight holes of two six-hole (½-cup/125ml) oval friand pans; line bases with baking paper.

2 Stir chocolate, butter, brown sugar, syrup and milk in a medium saucepan, over low heat, until smooth. Cool 15 minutes.

3 Whisk in sifted flours and egg. Stir in Choc Bits. Divide mixture into pan holes.

4 Bake cakes about 25 minutes. Stand cakes in pans 5 minutes before turning, top-side up, onto a wire rack to cool. Serve dusted with sifted icing sugar.

makes 18
prep + cook time
1 hour 15 minutes
(+ cooling & refrigeration)

jelly cakes

- 125g (4 ounces) butter, softened
- 1 teaspoon vanilla extract
- ½ cup (110g) caster (superfine) sugar
- 2 eggs
- 1½ cups (225g) self-raising flour
- ½ cup (125ml) milk
- 85g (3 ounce) packet raspberry jelly crystals
- 1 cup (250ml) boiling water
- 1 cup (250ml) cold water
- ½ cup (125ml) thickened (heavy) cream
- 1 tablespoon icing (confectioners') sugar
- 2 cups (160g) desiccated coconut, approximately

1 Preheat oven to 200°C/400°F. Grease 18 holes of two 12-hole gem irons.

2 Beat butter, extract and sugar in a small bowl with an electric mixer until light and fluffy; beat in eggs one at a time, beating until combined. Stir in sifted flour and milk. Drop tablespoons of mixture into gem irons.

3 Bake cakes about 15 minutes. Turn cakes, top-side up, onto a wire rack to cool.

4 Meanwhile, dissolve jelly crystals in the boiling water, add the cold water, stir to combine; refrigerate for 45 minutes or until jelly is partly set.

5 Beat cream with icing sugar until firm peaks form.

6 Cut rounded tops from cakes. Join cakes with cream; dip in jelly, roll in coconut. Place on a tray; refrigerate 30 minutes.

Tips There are several different sizes and types of nut roll tins available. As a guide, the tins should be filled just a little over halfway.

fig jam & raisin rolls

- 125g (4 ounces) butter, softened
- ½ cup (100g) firmly packed brown sugar
- 2 eggs
- 1½ cups (225g) self-raising flour
- ½ cup (160g) fig jam
- 1 cup (170g) finely chopped raisins
- ½ cup (125ml) milk

1 Position oven racks to fit standing nut roll tins. Preheat oven to 180°C/350°F. Grease two 8cm x 19cm (3-inch x 8-inch) nut roll tins; line bases with baking paper. Place tins upright on an oven tray.

2 Beat butter and sugar in a small bowl with an electric mixer until light and fluffy. Add eggs, one at a time (mixture may curdle). Transfer mixture to a medium bowl. Stir in flour, jam, raisins and milk, in two batches. Spoon mixture into tins; top with lids.

3 Bake rolls about 50 minutes. Stand rolls 5 minutes, before removing ends (top and bottom); shake tins gently to release fruit rolls onto a wire rack to cool.

serving suggestion
Serve with butter or jam.

makes 20
prep + cook time
1 hour 15 minutes
(+ standing)

chewy chocolate slice

- 125g (4 ounces) butter, melted
- 1 cup (220g) firmly packed brown sugar
- 1 egg, beaten lightly
- 1 teaspoon vanilla extract
- ½ cup (75g) plain (all-purpose) flour
- ¼ cup (35g) self-raising flour
- 2 tablespoons cocoa powder
- ½ cup (40g) desiccated coconut
- 1 tablespoon desiccated coconut, extra

chocolate icing

- 10g (½ ounce) butter, melted
- 1½ tablespoons hot water, approximately
- 1 cup (160g) icing (confectioners') sugar
- 2 tablespoons cocoa powder

1 Preheat oven to 180°C/350°F. Grease a 20cm x 30cm (8-inch x 12-inch) slice pan; line with baking paper, extending paper 5cm (2-inches) over long sides.
2 Combine butter, sugar, egg and extract in a medium bowl. Stir in sifted flours and cocoa, then coconut. Spread mixture over base of pan.
3 Bake for 30 minutes or until slice is firm.
4 Meanwhile, make chocolate icing.
5 Spread hot slice with chocolate icing; sprinkle with extra coconut. Cool in pan before cutting.

chocolate icing
Combine butter and the water in a medium bowl; add sifted icing sugar and cocoa, stir until icing is spreadable.

tip Store slice in an airtight container for up to 1 week.

choc brownies with sour cream frosting

- 125g (4 ounces) butter, chopped
- 185g (6 ounces) dark (semi-sweet) chocolate, chopped
- 1 cup (220g) caster (superfine) sugar
- 2 teaspoons vanilla extract
- 2 eggs, beaten lightly
- 1 cup (150g) plain (all-purpose) flour
- ½ cup (60g) coarsely chopped pecans

sour cream frosting

- 100g (3 ounces) dark (semi-sweet) chocolate, chopped
- ¼ cup (60g) sour cream

1 Preheat oven to 180°C/350°F. Grease a deep 19cm (8-inch) square cake pan; line base with baking paper.

2 Place butter and chocolate in a small saucepan; stir over low heat until melted. Transfer mixture to a large bowl. Stir in sugar and extract, then eggs, sifted flour and nuts. Pour mixture into pan.

3 Bake for 30 minutes or until set; cool in pan.

4 Make sour cream frosting.

5 Turn brownie out of pan; spread top with frosting. Refrigerate until set before cutting.

sour cream frosting

Melt chocolate in a small heatproof bowl over a small saucepan of simmering water. Stir in sour cream; stir constantly until mixture is smooth and glossy.

tip Store slice, covered, in the refrigerator for up to 4 days.

makes 16
prep + cook time 55 minutes
(+ cooling & refrigeration)

apple ginger cakes with lemon icing

You will need one large apple (200g) for this recipe.

- 250g (8 ounces) butter, softened
- 1½ cups (330g) firmly packed dark brown sugar
- 3 eggs
- ¼ cup (90g) golden syrup or treacle
- 2 cups (300g) plain (all-purpose) flour
- 1½ teaspoons bicarbonate of soda (baking soda)
- 2 tablespoons ground ginger
- 1 tablespoon ground cinnamon
- 1 cup (170g) coarsely grated apple
- ⅔ cup (160ml) hot water

lemon icing
- 2 cups (320g) icing (confectioners') sugar
- 2 teaspoons butter, softened
- ⅓ cup (80ml) lemon juice

1 Preheat oven to 180°C/350°F. Grease two six-hole (¾-cup/180ml) mini fluted tube pans or texas muffin pans.
2 Beat butter and sugar in a small bowl with an electric mixer until light and fluffy. Beat in eggs, one at a time, then beat in syrup.
3 Transfer mixture to a medium bowl; stir in sifted dry ingredients, apple and the water. Divide mixture between pan holes; smooth tops.
4 Bake cakes about 25 minutes. Stand cakes in pans 5 minutes before turning, top-side up, onto a wire rack to cool.
5 Make lemon icing.
6 Drizzle lemon icing over cakes.

lemon icing
Sift icing sugar into a medium heatproof bowl; stir in butter and juice to form a paste. Stir over a medium saucepan of simmering water until icing is of a pouring consistency.

tip Store cakes in an airtight container for 3 days. Uniced cakes are suitable to freeze for up to 3 months.

melting moments

- 250g (8 ounces) butter, softened
- 1 teaspoon vanilla extract
- ½ cup (80g) icing (confectioners') sugar
- 1½ cups (225g) plain (all-purpose) flour
- ½ cup (75g) cornflour (cornstarch)

butter cream

- 90g (3 ounces) butter, softened
- ¾ cup (120g) icing (confectioners') sugar
- 1 teaspoon finely grated lemon rind
- 1 teaspoon lemon juice

1 Preheat oven to 160°C/325°F. Line oven trays with baking paper.
2 Beat butter, extract and icing sugar in a small bowl with an electric mixer until light and fluffy. Transfer mixture to a large bowl, stir in sifted flours in two batches.
3 With floured hands, roll rounded teaspoons of mixture into balls; place about 2.5cm (1-inch) apart on trays. Flatten slightly with a floured fork.

4 Bake biscuits about 15 minutes. Stand 5 minutes before lifting onto wire racks to cool.
5 Make butter cream.
6 Sandwich biscuits with butter cream. Dust with extra sifted icing sugar before serving.

butter cream

Beat butter, icing sugar and rind in a small bowl with an electric mixer until pale and fluffy; beat in juice.

makes 25
prep + cook time 40 minutes

Tip Filled biscuits will keep for a few days in an airtight container in the fridge. Unfilled biscuits will keep in an airtight container for up to a week.

vanilla passionfruit slice

- 1 sheet puff pastry
- ¼ cup (55g) caster (superfine) sugar
- ¼ cup (35g) cornflour (cornstarch)
- 1½ tablespoons custard powder (instant pudding mix)
- 1¼ cups (310ml) milk
- 30g (1 ounce) butter
- 1 egg yolk
- ½ teaspoon vanilla extract

passionfruit icing
- ¾ cup (120g) icing (confectioners') sugar
- 1 tablespoon passionfruit pulp
- 1 teaspoon water, approximately

makes 8
prep + cook time 45 minutes (+ cooling & refrigeration)

1 Preheat oven to 240°C/475°F. Grease an 8cm x 26cm (3¼-inch x 10½-inch) bar cake pan; line with a strip of foil extending over long sides of pan.

2 Place pastry sheet on an oven tray. Bake for 15 minutes or until puffed; cool. Split pastry in half horizontally; remove and discard any uncooked pastry from centre. Flatten pastry pieces gently with hand; trim both to fit pan. Place top half in pan, top-side down.

3 Meanwhile, combine sugar, cornflour and custard powder in a medium saucepan; gradually stir in milk. Stir over medium heat until mixture boils and thickens. Reduce heat; simmer, stirring, for 3 minutes or until custard is thick and smooth. Remove pan from heat; stir in butter, egg yolk and extract.

4 Spread hot custard over the pastry in pan; top with remaining pastry, bottom-side up, press down gently. Cool to room temperature.

5 Meanwhile, make passionfruit icing.

6 Spread pastry with icing; set at room temperature. Refrigerate 3 hours before cutting.

passionfruit icing
Sift icing sugar into a small heatproof bowl; stir in passionfruit and enough water to make a thick paste. Stir over a small saucepan of simmering water until icing is spreadable.

tip Slice can be made a day ahead, refrigerate in an airtight container.

ALMONDS flat, pointy-tipped nuts having a pitted brown shell enclosing a creamy white kernel that is covered by a brown skin.
flaked paper-thin slices.
ground also known as ground meal; nuts are powdered to a coarse flour texture for use in baking or as a thickening agent.
BAKING PAPER also known as parchment, silicon paper or non-stick baking paper; not to be confused with greaseproof or waxed paper. Used to line pans before cooking and baking.
BAKING POWDER a raising agent consisting mainly of two parts cream of tartar to one part bicarbonate of soda (baking soda).
BARBECUE SAUCE a spicy, tomato-based sauce used to baste or as a condiment.
BAY LEAVES aromatic leaves from the bay tree used to flavour soups, stocks and casseroles.
BEETROOT also known as red beets or beets; a firm, round root vegetable.
BICARBONATE OF SODA also known as baking soda; a mild alkali used as a leavening agent in baking.
BUTTER 125g is equal to 1 stick (4 ounces) butter. Use salted or unsalted according to the recipe directions; unsalted or 'sweet' butter has no added salt and is perhaps the most popular butter among pastry chefs.

BUTTERMILK originally the term given to the slightly sour liquid left after butter was churned from cream, today it is made from no-fat or low-fat milk to which specific bacterial cultures have been added. Sold alongside all fresh milk products in supermarkets; despite the implication of its name, it is low in fat.
CAPERS the grey-green buds of a warm climate (usually Mediterranean) shrub, sold either dried and salted or pickled in a vinegar brine. Baby capers, those picked early, are fuller-flavoured and more expensive than the full-sized ones. Whether packed in brine or in salt, capers must be rinsed well before using.
CHEESE
buffalo mozzarella a delicate, semi-soft, white cheese traditionally made from buffalo milk. Sold fresh, it spoils rapidly so will only keep, refrigerated in brine, for 1 or 2 days at the most.
cheddar the most common cow milk 'tasty' cheese; should be aged, hard and have a pronounced bite.
cream commonly called philadelphia or philly; a soft cow-milk cheese.
parmesan also called parmigiano; a hard, grainy cow-milk cheese originating in the Parma region of Italy. Aged for a minimum 2 years, Reggiano is the best variety.

pizza a blend of grated mozzarella, cheddar and parmesan cheeses.
CHICKEN BREAST FILLET skinned and boned.
CHIVES related to the onion and leek, with a subtle onion flavour. Used in sauces, dressings, omelettes or as a garnish.
CHOCOLATE
choc bits also known as chocolate chips or chocolate morsels; available in milk, white and dark chocolate. Made of cocoa liquor, cocoa butter, sugar and an emulsifier, and hold their shape in baking so are ideal for decorating.
dark also known as luxury or semi-sweet chocolate; made of a high percentage of cocoa liquor and cocoa butter, and a little added sugar.
white contains no cocoa solids but derives its sweet flavour from cocoa butter. It is very sensitive to heat, so watch carefully when melting.
CINNAMON the dried inner bark of the shoots of the cinnamon tree. Available as sticks (quills) or ground as a powder.
COCOA POWDER also called unsweetened cocoa. Cocoa beans (cacao seeds) are fermented, roasted, shelled and ground into powder then cleared of most of the fat content.
COCONUT, DESICCATED concentrated, dried, unsweetened and finely shredded coconut flesh.

glossary

CORNFLOUR also known as cornstarch. Available made from 100% corn or wheat; used as a thickening agent in cooking.

CREAM we use fresh cream, also known as pouring, single and pure cream; it has no additives.

sour a thick, commercially cultured soured cream.

thickened (heavy) a whipping cream containing a thickener.

CRÈME FRAÎCHE mature fermented cream having a slightly tangy, nutty flavour and velvety texture.

CUCUMBER, LEBANESE short, slender and thin-skinned. Probably the most popular variety because of its tender, edible skin, tiny, yielding seeds, and sweet, fresh and flavoursome taste.

CUSTARD POWDER instant mixture used to make pouring custard; similar to North American instant pudding mixes.

DILL also known as dill weed; used fresh or dried, in seed form or ground. Has an anise/celery sweetness flavour. Its feathery, frond-like fresh leaves are grassier and more subtle than the dried version or the seeds (which slightly resemble caraway in flavour).

FLOUR

plain also known as all-purpose; unbleached wheat flour is the best for baking: the gluten content ensures a strong dough, which produces a light result.

self-raising (rising) all-purpose plain or wholemeal flour with baking powder and salt added; can be made at home with plain or wholemeal flour sifted with baking powder in the proportion of 1 cup flour to 2 teaspoons baking powder.

GOLDEN SYRUP a by-product of refined sugarcane; pure maple syrup or honey can be substituted. Golden syrup and treacle (a thicker, darker syrup not unlike molasses), are also known as flavour syrups. Treacle is more viscous, and has a stronger flavour and aroma than golden syrup.

JELLY CRYSTALS a combination of sugar, gelatine, colours and flavours; when dissolved in water, the solution sets as firm jelly.

LEEK a member of the onion family; resembles the green shallot but is much larger.

LETTUCE, COS also known as romaine lettuce; the traditional Caesar salad lettuce.

MAYONNAISE we use mayonnaise made with whole eggs in our recipes.

MILK we use full-cream homogenised milk unless otherwise specified.

MUSTARD

dijon a pale brown, distinctively flavoured, fairly mild french mustard.

wholegrain also known as seeded. A french-style coarse-grain mustard made from crushed mustard seeds and dijon-style french mustard.

ONION, RED also known as Spanish, red Spanish or Bermuda onion; a sweet-flavoured, large, purple-red onion.

PANCETTA Italian bacon that is cured but not smoked. See prosciutto.

PARSLEY, FLAT-LEAF also known as continental parsley or italian parsley.

PASTRY

ready-rolled puff packaged sheets of frozen puff pastry, available from supermarkets.

ready-rolled shortcrust packaged sheets of frozen shortcrust pastry, available from supermarkets.

PINE NUTS also known as pignoli; not, in fact, a nut but a small, cream-coloured kernel from pine cones. Are best roasted before use to bring out the flavour.

POPPY SEEDS have a crunchy texture and a nutty flavour. Can be purchased whole or ground in most supermarkets.

PRAWNS (shrimp) varieties include school, king, royal red, Sydney harbour and tiger. Can be bought cooked or uncooked (green), with or without shells.

PROSCIUTTO an unsmoked Italian ham; salted, air-cured and aged, it is usually eaten uncooked. See pancetta.

ROCKET also known as arugula, rugula and rucola; a peppery-tasting green leaf which can be used similarly to baby spinach leaves; eaten raw in salads or cooked.

ROSEWATER distilled from rose petals, and used in the Middle East, North Africa, and India to flavour desserts. Not to be confused with rose essence, which is more concentrated.

SESAME SEEDS black and white are the most common of this small oval seed, however there are also red and brown varieties. Used as an ingredient and as a condiment. Roast the seeds in a heavy-based frying pan over low heat.

SUGAR we use coarse, granulated table sugar, also known as crystal sugar, unless otherwise specified.

brown an extremely soft, finely granulated sugar retaining molasses for its characteristic brown colour and flavour. Dark brown is a rich, moist, dark brown sugar. It contains more molasses than brown sugar.

caster also known as superfine or finely granulated table sugar. The fine crystals dissolve easily so it is perfect for cakes, meringues and desserts.

icing also known as confectioners' sugar or powdered sugar; pulverised granulated sugar crushed together with a small amount of cornflour.

SUMAC a purple-red, astringent spice ground from berries growing on shrubs around the Mediterranean; it has a tart, lemony flavour.

TEA

chai made by brewing black tea with a mixture of aromatic Indian spices and herbs. It is often drunk with milk. Spice milk tea from India (termed masala chai) exists in many varieties.

chamomile (camomile) a herbal tea made using the flowers of the chamomile plant, fresh or dried. Chamomile tea is used as a sedative.

darjeeling a tea from the Darjeeling district in West Bengal, India. It is available in black, green, white and oolong. When properly brewed, it yields a thin-bodied, light-coloured infusion with a floral aroma.

earl grey a tea blend with a distinctive smoky flavour and aroma derived from the addition of oil extracted from the rind of the bergamot orange, a fragrant citrus fruit.

english breakfast a traditional blend of black teas usually described as full-bodied, robust and rich. It is blended to go well with milk and sugar and is the most common form of tea in British tea culture.

green made from the leaves from the tea plant that have undergone minimal oxidation during processing. Green tea originated in China but it has become associated with many cultures throughout Asia.

rosehip the fruit of the rose plant, often blended with hibiscus.

THYME a member of the mint family, it has tiny grey-green leaves that give off a pungent light-lemon aroma. Fresh thyme should be stored in the refrigerator, wrapped in a damp paper towel and placed in a sealed bag for no more than a few days.

TREACLE thick, dark syrup not unlike molasses. See golden syrup.

TURKISH BREAD also known as pide. Sold in long (about 45cm) flat loaves as well as individual rounds; made from wheat flour and sprinkled with black onion seeds.

VANILLA EXTRACT obtained from vanilla beans infused in water or alcohol.

WATERCRESS one of a large group of peppery greens; used raw in salads, dips and sandwiches, or cooked in soups. Highly perishable, so must be used as soon as possible after purchase.

YEAST a raising agent used in dough making. Granular sachets and fresh compressed yeast can almost always be substituted one for the other.

YOGHURT, GREEK-STYLE full-cream yoghurt often made from sheep milk; the milk liquids are drained off leaving a thick, smooth consistency with a tart taste.

ZA'ATAR a blend of roasted dried spices, usually sesame seeds, wild marjoram, thyme and sumac; available in Middle-Eastern food and spice shops and delicatessens.

conversion chart

measures

One Australian metric measuring cup holds approximately 250ml, one Australian metric tablespoon holds 20ml, one Australian metric teaspoon holds 5ml. The difference between one country's measuring cups and another's is within a 2- or 3-teaspoon variance, and will not affect your cooking results. North America, New Zealand and the United Kingdom use a 15ml tablespoon. All cup and spoon measurements are level. The most accurate way of measuring dry ingredients is to weigh them. When measuring liquids, use a clear glass or plastic jug with metric markings. We use large eggs with an average weight of 60g.

dry measures

METRIC	IMPERIAL
15g	½oz
30g	1oz
60g	2oz
90g	3oz
125g	4oz (¼lb)
155g	5oz
185g	6oz
220g	7oz
250g	8oz (½lb)
280g	9oz
315g	10oz
345g	11oz
375g	12oz (¾lb)
410g	13oz
440g	14oz
470g	15oz
500g	16oz (1lb)
750g	24oz (1½lb)
1kg	32oz (2lb)

liquid measures

METRIC	IMPERIAL
30ml	1 fluid oz
60ml	2 fluid oz
100ml	3 fluid oz
125ml	4 fluid oz
150ml	5 fluid oz
190ml	6 fluid oz
250ml	8 fluid oz
300ml	10 fluid oz
500ml	16 fluid oz
600ml	20 fluid oz
1000ml (1 litre)	1¾ pints

length measures

METRIC	IMPERIAL
3mm	⅛in
6mm	¼in
1cm	½in
2cm	¾in
2.5cm	1in
5cm	2in
6cm	2½in
8cm	3in
10cm	4in
13cm	5in
15cm	6in
18cm	7in
20cm	8in
23cm	9in
25cm	10in
28cm	11in
30cm	12in (1ft)

oven temperatures

These oven temperatures are only a guide for conventional ovens. For fan-forced ovens, check the manufacturer's manual.

	°C (CELSIUS)	°F (FAHRENHEIT)
Very slow	120	250
Slow	150	275-300
Moderately slow	160	325
Moderate	180	350-375
Moderately hot	200	400
Hot	220	425-450
Very hot	240	475

The imperial measurements used in these recipes are approximate only. Measurements for cake pans are approximate only. Using same-shaped cake pans of a similar size should not affect the outcome of your baking. We measure the inside top of the cake pan to determine sizes.

index

This book is published in 2014 by Octopus Publishing Group Limited
based on materials licensed to it by Bauer Media Books, Australia
Bauer Media Books are published by Bauer Media Pty Limited
54 Park St, Sydney; GPO Box 4088, Sydney, NSW 2001, Australia
phone (+61) 2 9282 8618; fax (+61) 2 9126 3702
www.awwcookbooks.com.au

MEDIA GROUP

BAUER MEDIA BOOKS
Publisher - Jo Runciman
Editorial & Food Director - Pamela Clark
Director of Sales, Marketing & Rights - Brian Cearnes
Creative Director - Hieu Chi Nguyen
Art Director - Hannah Blackmore
Designer - Melissa Dumas
Senior Editor - Wendy Bryant
Junior Editor - Amy Bayliss
Food Concept Director - Sophia Young
Food Editor - Emma Braz

Published and Distributed in the United Kingdom by Octopus Publishing Group
Endeavour House
189 Shaftesbury Avenue
London WC2H 8JY
phone (+44)(0)207 632 5400; fax (+44)(0)207 632 5405
info@octopus-publishing.co.uk;
www.octopusbooks.co.uk

Printed by 1010 Printing International Limited in China.

International foreign language rights, Brian Cearnes, Bauer Media Books
bcearnes@bauer-media.com.au

A catalogue record for this book is available from the British Library.
ISBN: 978 1 74245 446 7
© Bauer Media Pty Limited 2014
ABN 18 053 273 546